WEALTH AFFIRMATIONS - UNLOCK ABUNDANCE AND FINANCIAL FREEDOM

Transform Your Financial Life with Daily Positive Affirmations

Vishal Anand

Vishal Anand Media

Copyright © 2024 Vishal Anand Media

No part of this publication may be copied, reproduced, distributed or transmitted in any form or by any means, including photocopying, recording, or other electronic or mechanical methods, without the prior written permission of the author, except for brief quotations used in reviews.

For permissions, please contact the publisher at:

www.theVishalAnand.com

OTHER IMPACTFUL BOOKS FROM THE AUTHOR

31 Life-Changing Habits and Behaviors Based on Science and Research to Build Unshakable Self-Confidence, Boost Self-Esteem, Strengthen Self-Worth, and Change Your Life
https://amzn.to/3YZVAOt

51 Habits That Are Keeping You Broke: Identify, Confront, and Change the Habits Draining Your Wallet
https://amzn.to/3CnPPRI

51 Procrastination Habits That Keep You Stuck: Identify, Confront, and Stop Procrastinating Forever
https://amzn.to/3O1Gx0k

51 Thoughts That Keep You Up at Night: Identify, Confront, and Quiet the Thoughts Stealing Your Peace and Sleep
https://amzn.to/40FRKeE

21 Timeless Laws and Principles for Lasting Success in Business and Life: Short Guide to Unlocking Proven Success Strategies for Business, Leadership, and Personal Growth
https://amzn.to/3ANbeTQ

Master Goals: A 7-Day Proven Plan to Slay Your Goals and Live Life on Your Terms
https://amzn.to/4fch3t7

Master Focus: A 7-Day Plan to Clarify Your Goals and Boost Your Focus for Maximum Productivity
https://amzn.to/4fl6EeK

Mindful Moments: 51 Inspirational Quotes, Real-Life Stories & Practices to Guide Your Path to Mindfulness, Wellbeing and Balance
https://amzn.to/4fxnlTY

Unf*ck Your Life in Thirty Days: Smash Fear, Build Courage and Take Charge of Your Life
https://amzn.to/3YJEQJL

CONTENTS

Title Page
Copyright
Other Impactful Books From The Author
Introduction: Unlock the Power of Your Wealth Mindset — 1
1: I Attract Wealth and Success — 4
2: I Embrace Opportunities for Growth — 6
3: I Deserve Financial Freedom — 8
4: Money Flows to Me Effortlessly — 10
5: I Am Open to New Streams of Income — 12
6: I Embrace Financial Abundance — 14
7: I Am Financially Empowered — 16
8: I Make Smart Financial Decisions — 18
9: I Am Worthy of Prosperity — 20
10: I Am Committed to My Financial Goals — 22
11: I Create Unlimited Wealth — 24
12: I Am Grateful for My Financial Blessings — 26
13: I Attract Lucrative Opportunities — 28
14: I Am a Successful Money Manager — 30

15: I Am Focused on Achieving Financial Freedom	32
16: I Believe in My Ability to Generate Wealth	34
17: I Am Aligned with the Energy of Abundance	36
18: I Welcome Financial Growth with Open Arms	38
19: I Am Persistent in Achieving My Financial Goals	40
20: I Radiate Wealth and Prosperity	42
21: I Attract Profitable Investments	44
22: I Am a Smart and Savvy Investor	46
23: I Deserve to Be Financially Rewarded	48
24: I Am a Beacon for Financial Success	50
25: I Handle Money with Wisdom and Grace	52
26: I Am Confident in My Financial Decisions	54
27: I Manifest Wealth Through My Actions	56
28: I Am Driven to Achieve Financial Excellence	58
29: I Attract Positive Financial Influences	60
30: I Am the Master of My Financial Destiny	62
31: I Create Value and Receive Abundance	64
32: I Am Dedicated to Building My Wealth	66
33: I Am Resilient in My Financial Journey	68
34: I Attract High-Paying Opportunities	70
35: I Am Financially Free and Secure	72
36: I Invest My Money Wisely	74
37: I Am Open to Receiving Financial Abundance	76
38: I Trust the Process of Wealth Creation	78
39: I Am a Powerful Money Magnet	80
40: I Attract Financial Miracles	82

41: I Am Committed to My Financial Growth	84
42: I Deserve to Live a Wealthy Life	86
43: I Am Attracting Financial Abundance Daily	88
44: I Am Financially Thriving	90
45: I Embrace a Wealth-Conscious Mindset	92
46: I Am a Creator of Financial Prosperity	94
47: I Attract Wealth Effortlessly	96
48: I Am in Control of My Financial Future	98
49: I Am Worthy of All the Wealth I Desire	100
50: I Am Continuously Attracting Financial Opportunities	102
Conclusion: Ignite Your Journey to Financial Freedom	104
Your Voice Matters — Leave a Review	107
Unlock Exclusive Free Tools & Articles!	109

INTRODUCTION: UNLOCK THE POWER OF YOUR WEALTH MINDSET

Welcome to Your Journey of Abundance

Welcome! You hold in your hands a powerful tool that can transform your financial destiny. **"Wealth Affirmations - Unlock Abundance and Financial Freedom"** is more than just a collection of positive statements—it's a guide backed by science, research, and countless success stories that have paved the way for financial prosperity.

The Science Behind Affirmations

Did you know that your thoughts can shape your reality? Studies in psychology and neuroscience have shown that positive affirmations can rewire your brain, enhancing your confidence, reducing stress, and improving decision-making. When you consistently practice these affirmations, you activate the parts of your brain that foster growth, resilience, and a proactive approach to financial success.

Stories of Transformation

Across the globe, people from all walks of life have used affirmations to break free from financial struggles and build lasting wealth. Take Sarah, who went from living paycheck to paycheck to owning her dream business, all by embracing daily affirmations that reinforced her worth and potential. Or James, who overcame significant debt and achieved financial independence by shifting his mindset and taking inspired actions. These stories prove that with the right mindset, anyone can achieve financial freedom.

What You Will Discover

Inside this book, you will uncover **50 unique affirmations** designed to:

- **Shift Your Mindset:** Replace limiting beliefs with empowering thoughts that attract wealth.
- **Enhance Your Confidence:** Build the self-assurance needed to pursue and seize financial opportunities.
- **Promote Financial Growth:** Implement actionable strategies that align with your wealth goals.
- **Foster Resilience:** Stay motivated and persistent, even when faced with challenges.

Each chapter is structured to provide you with a daily boost, the power behind the affirmation, actionable power moves, and quick reflections to keep you engaged and progressing toward your financial dreams.

How to Use This Book

This book is designed to be your constant companion on the path to financial freedom. You don't have to read it from start to finish. Instead, use it in a way that best fits your life:

- **Any Order:** Open any chapter that resonates with you at the moment. Whether you need a boost of confidence, motivation to take action, or a reminder of your worthiness, you'll find the right affirmation to inspire you.
- **Keep It Accessible:** Place this book on your side table, coffee table, in your purse, laptop bag, or office desk. Whenever you need a quick

dose of inspiration, you'll have it right at your fingertips.

- **Daily Practice:** Make it a habit to read your daily boost each morning to set a positive tone for the day. Use the reflections to track your progress and stay focused on your goals.

Ignite Your Financial Freedom Today

The journey to financial freedom begins with a single step—a belief in your ability to create and sustain wealth. By embracing the affirmations in this book, you are committing to a brighter, more prosperous future. Let these affirmations light the fire within you, inspiring you to take immediate and consistent action toward your financial goals.

Final Words of Encouragement

You have the power to change your financial story. Believe in yourself, stay dedicated, and let these affirmations guide you to the abundance and financial freedom you deserve. Remember, every great journey starts with a single step. Take that step today, and watch as your mindset transforms your financial reality.

"I am ready to embrace abundance and create the financial freedom I deserve."

Carry this affirmation with you, let it inspire your actions, and witness the incredible transformation that unfolds as you unlock the power of your wealth mindset.

1: I ATTRACT WEALTH AND SUCCESS

Your Daily Boost

"I attract wealth and success."

The Power Behind It

Attracting wealth and success begins with a positive and focused mindset. This affirmation helps you align your thoughts and actions with your financial aspirations. By believing in your ability to attract prosperity, you open yourself up to opportunities and strategies that lead to sustained wealth and achievement.

Power Moves to Make It Happen

1. Set Clear Intentions:

- **Define Success:** Clearly outline what wealth and success mean to you.
- **Write It Down:** Keep a journal of your financial and personal success goals.

2. Visualize Your Success:

- **Daily Visualization:** Spend a few minutes each day imagining yourself achieving your financial goals.
- **Create a Vision Board:** Use images and words that represent your wealth and success aspirations.

3. Take Consistent Action:

- **Daily Habits:** Develop daily habits that support

your financial goals, such as saving or investing.

- **Stay Persistent:** Keep working towards your goals, even when faced with challenges.

4. Maintain a Positive Attitude:

- **Positive Affirmations:** Use positive statements to reinforce your belief in attracting wealth and success.

- **Surround Yourself with Positivity:** Engage with positive people and environments that support your financial growth.

Quick Reflection

- *"What does wealth and success look like for you?"*

- *"What steps can you take today to move closer to attracting more wealth and success?"*

2: I EMBRACE OPPORTUNITIES FOR GROWTH

Your Daily Boost

"I embrace opportunities for growth."

The Power Behind It

Growth comes when you welcome new chances to learn and improve. By embracing opportunities, you open doors to financial success and personal development. This mindset helps you stay positive and ready to take on challenges that lead to abundance.

Power Moves to Make It Happen

1. Stay Curious:

   - **Ask Questions:** Whenever you encounter something new, ask questions to understand it better.
   - **Seek Knowledge:** Read books, attend workshops, or take online courses to expand your skills and knowledge.

2. Take Calculated Risks:

   - **Evaluate Opportunities:** Look at the potential benefits and drawbacks before making decisions.
   - **Step Out of Comfort Zone:** Try something you've never done before to grow your experience and confidence.

3. **Reflect on Experiences:**
    - **Daily Journaling:** Write down what you learned each day and how it can help you grow.
    - **Learn from Mistakes:** View setbacks as lessons that guide you toward future success.

4. **Network with Like-Minded People:**
    - **Join Groups:** Participate in communities or groups that focus on personal and financial growth.
    - **Share Ideas:** Exchange ideas and experiences with others to inspire and motivate each other.

Quick Reflection

- *"What new opportunity can you embrace this week to foster your growth?"*
- *"How have recent challenges helped you grow financially or personally?"*

3: I DESERVE FINANCIAL FREEDOM

Your Daily Boost

"I deserve financial freedom."

The Power Behind It

Believing that you deserve financial freedom is the first step toward achieving it. This affirmation helps you recognize your worth and your right to live a life free from financial stress. When you believe in your deservingness, you take actions that align with your financial goals.

Power Moves to Make It Happen

1. Affirm Your Worth:

- **Daily Affirmations:** Repeat, "I deserve financial freedom," every morning to reinforce your belief.
- **Positive Self-Talk:** Replace negative thoughts with positive ones that affirm your worthiness.

2. Set Clear Goals:

- **Define Financial Freedom:** Write down what financial freedom looks like for you.
- **Create a Plan:** Break down your goals into actionable steps to make them achievable.

3. Manage Your Finances Wisely:

- **Budgeting:** Create and stick to a budget to control your spending and save more.
- **Invest Smartly:** Learn about investment

options that can grow your wealth over time.

4. Surround Yourself with Support:

- **Find a Mentor:** Connect with someone who has achieved financial freedom for guidance and inspiration.
- **Join Support Groups:** Engage with communities that share your financial goals and can offer encouragement.

Quick Reflection

- *"In what ways do you acknowledge your right to financial freedom?"*
- *"What steps can you take today to move closer to your financial independence?"*

4: MONEY FLOWS TO ME EFFORTLESSLY

Your Daily Boost

"Money flows to me effortlessly."

The Power Behind It

When you believe that money flows to you effortlessly, you attract financial opportunities with ease. This affirmation helps you adopt a relaxed and open mindset towards wealth, making it easier to receive and manage money. Trusting the flow of money reduces stress and increases your ability to handle finances wisely.

Power Moves to Make It Happen

1. Cultivate an Abundance Mindset:

- **Focus on Plenty:** Remind yourself that there is enough money for everyone, including you.
- **Avoid Scarcity Thoughts:** Replace thoughts of lack with beliefs in abundance.

2. Practice Gratitude:

- **Daily Gratitude List:** Write down things you're grateful for, especially related to money.
- **Appreciate Small Wins:** Celebrate even the smallest financial successes.

3. Take Inspired Action:

- **Follow Intuition:** Act on ideas that feel right and aligned with your financial goals.

- **Be Proactive:** Look for and create opportunities that can bring in money effortlessly.

4. Simplify Your Finances:

- **Automate Savings:** Set up automatic transfers to your savings or investment accounts.
- **Streamline Expenses:** Reduce unnecessary expenses to allow money to flow more freely.

Quick Reflection

- *"How can you create more ease in your financial life today?"*
- *"What positive changes have you noticed since believing that money flows effortlessly to you?"*

5: I AM OPEN TO NEW STREAMS OF INCOME

Your Daily Boost

"I am open to new streams of income."

The Power Behind It

Being open to new streams of income allows you to diversify your earnings and increase your financial security. This affirmation encourages you to explore different ways to make money, whether through side jobs, investments, or passive income sources. Embracing multiple income streams can accelerate your journey to financial freedom.

Power Moves to Make It Happen

1. Explore Side Hustles:

- **Identify Skills:** Think about what you're good at and how you can monetize those skills.
- **Start Small:** Begin with a manageable side project that fits your schedule.

2. Invest Wisely:

- **Learn About Investments:** Educate yourself on stocks, real estate, or other investment opportunities.
- **Diversify Portfolio:** Spread your investments to minimize risks and maximize potential returns.

3. Create Passive Income:

- **Digital Products:** Develop e-books, online courses, or other digital products that can generate income over time.
- **Rental Income:** Consider investing in property to earn rental income.

4. Network and Collaborate:

- **Connect with Entrepreneurs:** Build relationships with people who have multiple income streams.
- **Partner Up:** Collaborate on projects or business ventures that can create additional income sources.

Quick Reflection

- *"What new income opportunity can you explore this month?"*
- *"How can you leverage your existing skills to create an additional income stream?"*

6: I EMBRACE FINANCIAL ABUNDANCE

Your Daily Boost

"I embrace financial abundance."

The Power Behind It

Embracing financial abundance means opening your heart and mind to the wealth that surrounds you. This affirmation helps you recognize and accept the limitless opportunities for prosperity in your life. By welcoming abundance, you shift your mindset from one of scarcity to one of plenty, allowing you to attract and receive wealth more freely.

Power Moves to Make It Happen

1. **Cultivate an Abundance Mindset:**
   - *Shift Your Focus:* Concentrate on what you have rather than what you lack.
   - *Positive Language:* Use affirming words when talking about your finances.
2. **Practice Daily Gratitude:**
   - *Gratitude Journal:* Write down three things you're grateful for each day, especially related to wealth and prosperity.
   - *Express Appreciation:* Thank others for their contributions to your financial journey.

3. **Visualize Abundance:**
   - *Guided Imagery:* Spend time each day visualizing yourself living in financial abundance.
   - *Create a Vision Board:* Assemble images and words that represent financial prosperity to inspire and motivate you.
4. **Eliminate Scarcity Beliefs:**
   - *Identify Limiting Thoughts:* Recognize and challenge beliefs that suggest there's not enough to go around.
   - *Affirm Plenty:* Remind yourself regularly that the universe is abundant and there's more than enough for everyone.

Quick Reflection

- "In what ways can I acknowledge and embrace the financial abundance already present in my life?"

- "What limiting beliefs about money can I let go of to allow more abundance to flow to me?"

7: I AM FINANCIALLY EMPOWERED

Your Daily Boost

"I am financially empowered."

The Power Behind It

Feeling financially empowered means having control over your financial situation and making informed decisions. This affirmation boosts your confidence in managing money, setting and achieving financial goals, and overcoming financial challenges. Empowerment leads to greater financial stability and independence.

Power Moves to Make It Happen

1. **Educate Yourself:**

    - **Financial Literacy:** Read books or take courses on personal finance and money management.
    - **Stay Informed:** Keep up with financial news and trends to make informed decisions.

2. **Create a Budget:**

    - **Track Expenses:** Monitor where your money goes each month.
    - **Set Limits:** Allocate funds for different categories and stick to your budget.

3. **Build an Emergency Fund:**

    - **Save Regularly:** Set aside a portion of your income for unexpected expenses.
    - **Set Goals:** Aim to save at least three to six

months' worth of living expenses.

4. Make Informed Decisions:

- **Research Before Spending:** Think carefully before making large purchases or investments.

- **Seek Professional Advice:** Consult with financial advisors when needed to guide your decisions.

Quick Reflection

- *"How do you feel more in control of your finances today?"*

- *"What financial decision can you make this week that empowers you?"*

8: I MAKE SMART FINANCIAL DECISIONS

Your Daily Boost

"I make smart financial decisions."

The Power Behind It

Making smart financial decisions is crucial for building and maintaining wealth. This affirmation reinforces your ability to choose wisely regarding spending, saving, and investing. By committing to intelligent financial choices, you pave the way for long-term financial stability and growth.

Power Moves to Make It Happen

1. Set Financial Goals:
   - **Short-Term Goals:** Identify immediate financial objectives, like saving for a trip.
   - **Long-Term Goals:** Plan for future needs, such as retirement or buying a home.

2. Prioritize Spending:
   - **Needs vs. Wants:** Differentiate between essential expenses and discretionary spending.
   - **Value-Based Spending:** Allocate money to things that truly matter to you.

3. Monitor Your Finances:
   - **Regular Reviews:** Check your financial status monthly to stay on track.

- **Use Tools:** Utilize budgeting apps or spreadsheets to manage your money effectively.

4. Seek Knowledge:

- **Financial Education:** Continuously learn about personal finance, investments, and money management.
- **Consult Experts:** Don't hesitate to ask for advice from financial professionals when needed.

Quick Reflection

- *"What recent financial decision are you proud of?"*
- *"How can you improve your decision-making process to achieve better financial outcomes?"*

9: I AM WORTHY OF PROSPERITY

Your Daily Boost

"I am worthy of prosperity."

The Power Behind It

Believing that you are worthy of prosperity is essential for attracting and maintaining wealth. This affirmation helps you recognize your value and opens your mind to receiving abundance. When you feel worthy, you are more likely to pursue opportunities and make choices that lead to a prosperous life.

Power Moves to Make It Happen

1. **Self-Acceptance:**

   - **Embrace Yourself:** Accept and love yourself as you are, recognizing your strengths and achievements.
   - **Positive Self-Image:** Maintain a positive view of yourself and your abilities.

2. **Set High Standards:**

   - **Aim High:** Set ambitious financial goals that reflect your worth.
   - **Don't Settle:** Strive for what you deserve and avoid accepting less than your true value.

3. **Invest in Yourself:**

   - **Personal Development:** Spend time and resources on activities that enhance your skills and knowledge.

- **Health and Well-Being:** Take care of your physical and mental health to support your prosperity.

4. **Celebrate Successes:**

    - **Acknowledge Achievements:** Recognize and celebrate your financial milestones.
    - **Reward Yourself:** Treat yourself when you reach your goals to reinforce your worthiness.

Quick Reflection

- *"In what ways do you honor your worthiness of prosperity?"*
- *"What actions can you take today to reinforce your belief in your deservingness of wealth?"*

10: I AM COMMITTED TO MY FINANCIAL GOALS

Your Daily Boost

"I am committed to my financial goals."

The Power Behind It

Commitment to your financial goals ensures that you stay focused and persistent in your pursuit of wealth. This affirmation strengthens your dedication and motivates you to overcome obstacles. By being committed, you create a clear path toward achieving your financial dreams and securing your future.

Power Moves to Make It Happen

1. Define Your Goals Clearly:

- **Specificity:** Make your financial goals specific and measurable.
- **Timeline:** Set deadlines to create a sense of urgency and accountability.

2. Create an Action Plan:

- **Break It Down:** Divide your goals into smaller, manageable tasks.
- **Prioritize Tasks:** Focus on the most important actions that will move you closer to your goals.

3. Stay Accountable:

- **Track Progress:** Regularly review your progress toward your financial goals.

- **Find an Accountability Partner:** Share your goals with someone who can support and encourage you.

4. **Stay Motivated:**
   - **Visual Reminders:** Keep reminders of your goals where you can see them daily.
   - **Celebrate Milestones:** Reward yourself for reaching important milestones along the way.

Quick Reflection

- *"What financial goal are you most committed to right now?"*

- *"How can you strengthen your dedication to achieving your financial objectives?"*

11: I CREATE UNLIMITED WEALTH

Your Daily Boost

"I create unlimited wealth."

The Power Behind It

Believing that you can create unlimited wealth opens your mind to endless possibilities. This affirmation empowers you to think beyond limitations and take proactive steps toward financial abundance. When you embrace this mindset, you attract opportunities that help you build and sustain wealth effortlessly.

Power Moves to Make It Happen

1. **Set Clear Financial Goals:**

    - **Define Your Wealth:** Clearly outline what unlimited wealth means to you.
    - **Create a Plan:** Break down your goals into actionable steps to achieve them.

2. **Invest in Education:**

    - **Learn Continuously:** Read books, attend seminars, and take courses on wealth creation.
    - **Apply Knowledge:** Implement the strategies you learn to grow your finances.

3. **Diversify Income Streams:**

    - **Explore Opportunities:** Look for different ways to earn money, such as investments, side businesses, or passive income.

- **Balance Risk:** Spread your investments to minimize risks and maximize returns.

4. **Stay Positive and Persistent:**
    - **Maintain Optimism:** Keep a positive attitude even when faced with challenges.
    - **Be Consistent:** Regularly work towards your financial goals without giving up.

Quick Reflection

- *"What steps can you take today to start creating unlimited wealth?"*
- *"How can you diversify your income to support your financial goals?"*

12: I AM GRATEFUL FOR MY FINANCIAL BLESSINGS

Your Daily Boost

"I am grateful for my financial blessings."

The Power Behind It

Gratitude shifts your focus from what you lack to what you have, attracting more financial blessings into your life. This affirmation helps you appreciate your current financial situation, no matter how small, and opens the door for greater abundance. When you acknowledge your blessings, you invite more prosperity and joy.

Power Moves to Make It Happen

1. Keep a Gratitude Journal:

- **Daily Entries:** Write down at least three financial blessings each day.
- **Reflect Regularly:** Review your entries to stay focused on your blessings.

2. Express Thanks:

- **Share Gratitude:** Tell someone you're thankful for their support or assistance.
- **Celebrate Wins:** Acknowledge and celebrate your financial achievements, big or small.

3. Practice Mindfulness:

- **Stay Present:** Focus on the current financial blessings instead of worrying about the future.

- **Appreciate Now:** Take time to enjoy and appreciate what you have today.

4. **Reinforce Positive Thoughts:**
    - **Affirm Daily:** Repeat your gratitude affirmation every morning and night.
    - **Positive Visualization:** Imagine receiving more financial blessings and feel thankful for them.

Quick Reflection

- *"What financial blessings are you most grateful for today?"*
- *"How does practicing gratitude impact your financial mindset?"*

13: I ATTRACT LUCRATIVE OPPORTUNITIES

Your Daily Boost

"I attract lucrative opportunities."

The Power Behind It

Attracting lucrative opportunities means being open and ready to seize financial chances that come your way. This affirmation helps you stay alert and proactive in recognizing and pursuing profitable ventures. By believing in your ability to attract valuable opportunities, you enhance your potential for financial growth and success.

Power Moves to Make It Happen

1. Network Actively:

    - **Connect with Professionals:** Attend events and join groups related to your interests and goals.
    - **Build Relationships:** Foster genuine connections that can lead to new opportunities.

2. Stay Informed:

    - **Research Trends:** Keep up with industry trends and market changes to spot potential opportunities.
    - **Continuous Learning:** Educate yourself about different fields to diversify your knowledge.

3. Take Initiative:

- **Propose Ideas:** Don't wait for opportunities to come; create them by suggesting new projects or ventures.
- **Be Proactive:** Actively seek out opportunities instead of passively waiting for them.

4. Maintain a Positive Attitude:

- **Stay Optimistic:** Believe that good opportunities are available and within your reach.
- **Overcome Fear:** Push past doubts and take calculated risks to pursue lucrative ventures.

Quick Reflection

- *"What lucrative opportunity can you pursue this week?"*
- *"How can you expand your network to attract more financial opportunities?"*

14: I AM A SUCCESSFUL MONEY MANAGER

Your Daily Boost

"I am a successful money manager."

The Power Behind It

Being a successful money manager means effectively handling your finances to achieve your goals. This affirmation reinforces your ability to budget, save, and invest wisely. When you manage your money well, you build a strong foundation for financial stability and growth, leading to long-term success.

Power Moves to Make It Happen

1. Create a Budget:

- **Track Expenses:** Monitor where your money goes each month.
- **Allocate Funds:** Assign specific amounts for necessities, savings, and discretionary spending.

2. Save Regularly:

- **Automate Savings:** Set up automatic transfers to your savings account.
- **Set Savings Goals:** Define short-term and long-term savings targets.

3. Invest Wisely:

- **Diversify Investments:** Spread your

investments across different assets to minimize risk.

- **Research Opportunities:** Educate yourself about various investment options before committing.

4. **Monitor Financial Health:**

- **Review Statements:** Regularly check your bank and investment statements for accuracy.

- **Adjust as Needed:** Make changes to your budget and investments based on your financial situation.

Quick Reflection

- *"How effectively are you managing your current finances?"*

- *"What changes can you make to improve your money management skills?"*

15: I AM FOCUSED ON ACHIEVING FINANCIAL FREEDOM

Your Daily Boost

"I am focused on achieving financial freedom."

The Power Behind It

Focusing on financial freedom keeps your goals clear and your actions aligned towards achieving independence from financial stress. This affirmation helps you prioritize your financial objectives and stay committed to your path. By maintaining focus, you enhance your ability to make decisions that lead to long-term prosperity and freedom.

Power Moves to Make It Happen

1. Define Financial Freedom:

- **Clarify Your Vision:** Understand what financial freedom means to you personally.
- **Set Specific Goals:** Outline the steps needed to reach your financial independence.

2. Eliminate Debt:

- **Pay Off High-Interest Debt:** Focus on reducing debts that cost you the most.
- **Create a Debt Repayment Plan:** Strategize how to systematically eliminate your debts.

3. Increase Your Income:

- **Seek Promotions:** Aim for advancements in your current job.

- **Explore Side Gigs:** Take on additional work to boost your income.

4. Stay Disciplined:

- **Avoid Unnecessary Spending:** Stick to your budget and avoid impulse purchases.
- **Monitor Progress:** Regularly review your financial goals and adjust your strategies as needed.

Quick Reflection

- *"What does financial freedom look like for you?"*
- *"How can you stay focused and disciplined on your path to financial independence?"*

16: I BELIEVE IN MY ABILITY TO GENERATE WEALTH

Your Daily Boost

"I believe in my ability to generate wealth."

The Power Behind It

Believing in your ability to generate wealth is crucial for taking the necessary actions to build your financial future. This affirmation strengthens your confidence and motivates you to pursue opportunities that can increase your wealth. When you trust in your capabilities, you are more likely to take risks and make decisions that lead to financial success.

Power Moves to Make It Happen

1. Build Confidence:

- **Acknowledge Achievements:** Celebrate your financial successes, no matter how small.
- **Positive Self-Talk:** Replace doubts with affirmations that reinforce your ability to generate wealth.

2. Set Ambitious Goals:

- **Dream Big:** Don't limit your financial aspirations; aim high.
- **Create a Plan:** Develop a step-by-step plan to achieve your wealth generation goals.

3. Take Action:

- **Start Investing:** Begin investing in areas that interest you and have growth potential.
- **Launch a Business:** Consider starting your own business to create additional income streams.

4. Learn from Others:

- **Find a Mentor:** Seek guidance from someone who has successfully generated wealth.
- **Study Success Stories:** Learn from the experiences and strategies of wealthy individuals.

Quick Reflection

- *"How does believing in your ability to generate wealth influence your financial decisions?"*
- *"What actions can you take today to strengthen your belief in your wealth-generating abilities?"*

17: I AM ALIGNED WITH THE ENERGY OF ABUNDANCE

Your Daily Boost

"I am aligned with the energy of abundance."

The Power Behind It

Being aligned with the energy of abundance means embracing a mindset that attracts prosperity and positive financial experiences. This affirmation helps you resonate with abundance, making it easier to attract wealth and opportunities. When your energy aligns with abundance, you naturally draw in the resources needed to support your financial goals.

Power Moves to Make It Happen

1. Practice Daily Affirmations:

- **Consistent Repetition:** Repeat your abundance affirmation every morning and evening.
- **Feel the Meaning:** Truly believe and feel the affirmation as you say it.

2. Surround Yourself with Abundance:

- **Positive Environment:** Keep your space filled with symbols of abundance, such as inspiring quotes or images.
- **Connect with Abundant People:** Engage with individuals who have an abundant mindset.

3. Let Go of Limiting Beliefs:

- **Identify Blocks:** Recognize and address any negative beliefs about money and abundance.
- **Replace with Positivity:** Substitute limiting thoughts with empowering ones that support abundance.

4. Give and Receive Generously:

- **Share Wealth:** Donate to causes you care about or help others financially when you can.
- **Accept Help:** Be open to receiving support and opportunities from others.

Quick Reflection

- "How does aligning with the energy of abundance change your financial outlook?"
- "What limiting beliefs can you release to embrace abundance more fully?"

18: I WELCOME FINANCIAL GROWTH WITH OPEN ARMS

Your Daily Boost

"I welcome financial growth with open arms."

The Power Behind It

Welcoming financial growth means being open to increasing your wealth and embracing the changes that come with it. This affirmation encourages you to accept and pursue opportunities that enhance your financial situation. By welcoming growth, you create a positive environment for your finances to flourish and evolve.

Power Moves to Make It Happen

1. Stay Open to Change:

- **Embrace New Ideas:** Be willing to try new financial strategies and approaches.
- **Adaptability:** Adjust your plans as needed to accommodate new opportunities.

2. Invest in Personal Development:

- **Enhance Skills:** Take courses or attend workshops to improve your financial knowledge.
- **Seek Feedback:** Learn from others to refine your financial strategies.

3. Expand Your Horizons:

- **Explore New Markets:** Look into different

industries or investment opportunities.

- **Diversify Investments:** Spread your investments to include various asset classes for growth.

4. Celebrate Growth:

- **Acknowledge Progress:** Recognize and celebrate each step of your financial growth journey.
- **Reward Yourself:** Treat yourself when you reach financial milestones to reinforce positive behavior.

Quick Reflection

- *"What new financial growth opportunities can you embrace this month?"*
- *"How can you stay open and adaptable to achieve continuous financial growth?"*

19: I AM PERSISTENT IN ACHIEVING MY FINANCIAL GOALS

Your Daily Boost

"I am persistent in achieving my financial goals."

The Power Behind It

Persistence is key to overcoming obstacles and staying on track toward your financial objectives. This affirmation reinforces your determination and resilience in the face of challenges. By being persistent, you ensure that setbacks do not derail your progress, keeping you focused on achieving your financial dreams.

Power Moves to Make It Happen

1. Stay Committed:

- **Daily Focus:** Remind yourself of your financial goals every day.
- **Avoid Distractions:** Stay focused on tasks that contribute to your financial success.

2. Overcome Obstacles:

- **Problem-Solving:** Identify challenges and develop strategies to overcome them.
- **Stay Positive:** Maintain a positive attitude, even when facing difficulties.

3. Track Your Progress:

- **Regular Check-Ins:** Monitor your progress toward your financial goals regularly.

- **Adjust as Needed:** Make necessary adjustments to your plans based on your progress.

4. Seek Support:

    - **Find a Mentor:** Connect with someone who can guide and encourage you.
    - **Join a Community:** Engage with like-minded individuals who share your financial aspirations.

Quick Reflection

- *"How does your persistence help you move closer to your financial goals?"*
- *"What strategies can you use to stay persistent during challenging times?"*

20: I RADIATE WEALTH AND PROSPERITY

Your Daily Boost

"I radiate wealth and prosperity."

The Power Behind It

Radiating wealth and prosperity means exuding confidence and positivity about your financial status. This affirmation helps you project an abundant mindset, attracting more wealth and prosperity into your life. When you radiate wealth, you create an environment that supports financial growth and success.

Power Moves to Make It Happen

1. Maintain a Positive Image:

- **Dress for Success:** Wear clothes that make you feel confident and successful.
- **Positive Body Language:** Use gestures and expressions that reflect confidence and abundance.

2. Practice Self-Care:

- **Healthy Lifestyle:** Take care of your physical and mental well-being to maintain high energy levels.
- **Stress Management:** Use techniques like meditation or exercise to reduce financial stress.

3. **Share Your Success:**

    - **Help Others:** Share your knowledge and resources with those in need.

    - **Celebrate Together:** Acknowledge and celebrate the successes of others to create a positive atmosphere.

4. **Visualize Prosperity:**

    - **Daily Visualization:** Imagine yourself living a prosperous life and feel the emotions associated with it.

    - **Affirm Wealth:** Regularly repeat wealth affirmations to reinforce your prosperous mindset.

Quick Reflection

- *"How do you embody wealth and prosperity in your daily life?"*

- *"What actions can you take to enhance the way you radiate abundance?"*

21: I ATTRACT PROFITABLE INVESTMENTS

Your Daily Boost

"I attract profitable investments."

The Power Behind It

Believing that you attract profitable investments opens doors to opportunities that can grow your wealth. This affirmation helps you stay open to smart investment choices and guides you toward financial growth. With this mindset, you become more attentive to lucrative opportunities that can enhance your financial future.

Power Moves to Make It Happen

1. Educate Yourself on Investments:

- **Learn the Basics:** Read books or take courses about different types of investments like stocks, real estate, and mutual funds.
- **Stay Updated:** Keep up with the latest market trends and news to make informed decisions.

2. Set Clear Investment Goals:

- **Define Your Objectives:** Decide what you want to achieve with your investments, whether it's saving for retirement, buying a home, or growing your wealth.
- **Create a Plan:** Outline the steps you need to take to reach your investment goals.

3. **Diversify Your Portfolio:**
    - **Spread Your Investments:** Invest in a variety of assets to reduce risk and increase potential returns.
    - **Balance Risk and Reward:** Choose a mix of safe and high-risk investments that align with your financial goals.
4. **Seek Professional Advice:**
    - **Consult Experts:** Talk to financial advisors who can provide guidance tailored to your investment strategy.
    - **Join Investment Groups:** Engage with communities of investors to share knowledge and experiences.

Quick Reflection

- *"What types of investments are you most interested in exploring?"*
- *"How can you start diversifying your investment portfolio today?"*

22: I AM A SMART AND SAVVY INVESTOR

Your Daily Boost

"I am a smart and savvy investor."

The Power Behind It

Being a smart and savvy investor means making informed and strategic decisions with your money. This affirmation boosts your confidence in navigating the investment world and helps you identify opportunities that align with your financial goals. With this mindset, you approach investments with wisdom and clarity, leading to better financial outcomes.

Power Moves to Make It Happen

1. Conduct Thorough Research:

- **Analyze Opportunities:** Before investing, research the potential risks and rewards.
- **Understand the Market:** Stay informed about market conditions and how they affect your investments.

2. Develop a Strategic Plan:

- **Set Clear Goals:** Define what you want to achieve with your investments.
- **Create a Timeline:** Establish when you aim to reach your investment milestones.

3. Monitor Your Investments:

- **Regular Reviews:** Keep track of your investment performance and make adjustments as needed.
- **Stay Informed:** Keep up with news and trends that may impact your investments.

4. Learn from Experience:

- **Reflect on Successes and Mistakes:** Use past experiences to improve your investment strategies.
- **Stay Adaptable:** Be willing to change your approach based on new information and market changes.

Quick Reflection

- *"What strategies do you use to make informed investment decisions?"*
- *"How can you enhance your investment knowledge to become even savvier?"*

23: I DESERVE TO BE FINANCIALLY REWARDED

Your Daily Boost

"I deserve to be financially rewarded."

The Power Behind It

Recognizing that you deserve financial rewards reinforces your self-worth and motivates you to pursue opportunities that bring abundance. This affirmation helps you embrace the belief that your efforts and talents are worthy of financial success. When you feel deserving, you are more likely to take actions that lead to financial rewards and prosperity.

Power Moves to Make It Happen

1. Acknowledge Your Achievements:

- **Celebrate Successes:** Take time to recognize and reward yourself for your financial milestones.
- **Keep a Success Journal:** Document your financial wins to remind yourself of your deservingness.

2. Set High Standards:

- **Aim for Excellence:** Strive to perform your best in all financial endeavors.
- **Avoid Settling:** Don't accept less than what you deserve in your financial agreements and opportunities.

3. **Invest in Self-Improvement:**
    - **Enhance Your Skills:** Take courses or attend workshops to improve your financial knowledge and abilities.
    - **Seek Feedback:** Learn from others to grow and become more financially competent.
4. **Affirm Your Worth Daily:**
    - **Positive Self-Talk:** Remind yourself daily that you deserve financial rewards.
    - **Visualize Success:** Imagine yourself receiving and enjoying financial rewards from your efforts.

Quick Reflection
- *"What financial achievements are you most proud of?"*
- *"How can you reinforce your belief that you deserve financial rewards?"*

24: I AM A BEACON FOR FINANCIAL SUCCESS

Your Daily Boost

"I am a beacon for financial success."

The Power Behind It

Being a beacon for financial success means you naturally attract prosperity and inspire others with your financial achievements. This affirmation strengthens your role as a leader in your financial journey, guiding you and those around you toward success. With this mindset, you become a source of motivation and positivity in the pursuit of financial goals.

Power Moves to Make It Happen

1. Lead by Example:

- **Demonstrate Good Habits:** Show others how to manage money wisely through your actions.
- **Share Your Journey:** Talk about your financial successes and challenges to inspire others.

2. Set Clear Financial Goals:

- **Define Success:** Clearly outline what financial success looks like for you.
- **Create a Roadmap:** Develop a step-by-step plan to achieve your financial objectives.

3. Stay Positive and Motivated:

- **Maintain Optimism:** Keep a positive attitude

even when faced with financial setbacks.

- **Find Inspiration:** Surround yourself with success stories and motivational resources.

4. **Support Others:**

    - **Offer Guidance:** Help others understand financial concepts and strategies.
    - **Build a Community:** Create or join groups that focus on financial success and mutual support.

Quick Reflection

- *"How can you inspire others with your financial success?"*
- *"What steps can you take to become a stronger beacon for financial achievement?"*

25: I HANDLE MONEY WITH WISDOM AND GRACE

Your Daily Boost

"I handle money with wisdom and grace."

The Power Behind It

Handling money with wisdom and grace means managing your finances thoughtfully and respectfully. This affirmation encourages you to make prudent financial decisions while maintaining a balanced and peaceful approach to money management. With this mindset, you create a harmonious relationship with your finances, leading to sustainable wealth and inner peace.

Power Moves to Make It Happen

1. Create a Budget:

- **Track Your Spending:** Monitor where your money goes each month to make informed decisions.
- **Allocate Wisely:** Assign specific amounts for necessities, savings, and discretionary spending.

2. Practice Mindful Spending:

- **Think Before You Buy:** Consider the value and necessity of each purchase.
- **Avoid Impulse Purchases:** Wait before making non-essential buys to ensure they align with your financial goals.

3. **Save and Invest Regularly:**
   - **Automate Savings:** Set up automatic transfers to your savings and investment accounts.
   - **Plan for the Future:** Invest in opportunities that will grow your wealth over time.

4. **Seek Financial Education:**
   - **Learn Continuously:** Educate yourself about personal finance and money management.
   - **Apply Knowledge:** Use what you learn to make smarter financial choices.

Quick Reflection
   - *"How do you ensure your spending aligns with your financial goals?"*
   - *"What practices help you manage your money with wisdom and grace?"*

26: I AM CONFIDENT IN MY FINANCIAL DECISIONS

Your Daily Boost

"I am confident in my financial decisions."

The Power Behind It

Confidence in your financial decisions empowers you to take control of your financial future. This affirmation helps you trust your judgment and make choices that align with your goals. When you believe in your ability to make sound financial decisions, you navigate money matters with assurance and clarity, leading to greater financial stability and success.

Power Moves to Make It Happen

1. Trust Your Knowledge:

- **Educate Yourself:** Gain a solid understanding of financial principles and strategies.
- **Stay Informed:** Keep up with financial news and trends to make informed decisions.

2. Set Clear Goals:

- **Define Your Objectives:** Know what you want to achieve financially.
- **Create a Plan:** Develop a roadmap to reach your financial goals with confidence.

3. Reflect on Past Successes:

- **Review Achievements:** Look back at financial

decisions that worked well for you.

- **Learn from Mistakes:** Understand what didn't work and how to improve.

4. Seek Support When Needed:

- **Consult Experts:** Don't hesitate to seek advice from financial advisors.
- **Join Support Groups:** Engage with communities that support your financial journey.

Quick Reflection

- *"What recent financial decision are you proud of?"*
- *"How does your confidence impact your financial choices?"*

27: I MANIFEST WEALTH THROUGH MY ACTIONS

Your Daily Boost

"I manifest wealth through my actions."

The Power Behind It

Manifesting wealth through your actions means that your daily behaviors and decisions are aligned with your financial goals. This affirmation encourages you to take proactive steps toward building wealth, ensuring that your actions reflect your desire for abundance. With this mindset, you create tangible results that lead to financial prosperity.

Power Moves to Make It Happen

1. Take Consistent Action:

- **Daily Habits:** Develop routines that support your financial goals, such as saving or investing regularly.
- **Stay Persistent:** Keep working towards your goals, even when progress seems slow.

2. Set Achievable Goals:

- **Break It Down:** Divide your financial goals into smaller, manageable tasks.
- **Track Progress:** Monitor your achievements to stay motivated and focused.

3. Invest in Yourself:

- **Enhance Skills:** Improve your abilities to increase your earning potential.
- **Personal Development:** Engage in activities that boost your confidence and productivity.

4. **Stay Positive and Focused:**
   - **Maintain Optimism:** Keep a positive attitude towards your financial journey.
   - **Avoid Negativity:** Steer clear of negative thoughts and focus on what you can achieve.

Quick Reflection

- *"What actions are you taking today to manifest wealth?"*
- *"How do your daily habits contribute to your financial goals?"*

28: I AM DRIVEN TO ACHIEVE FINANCIAL EXCELLENCE

Your Daily Boost

"I am driven to achieve financial excellence."

The Power Behind It

Being driven to achieve financial excellence means you are highly motivated to reach the highest standards in your financial life. This affirmation fuels your ambition and dedication to mastering money management and growing your wealth. With this mindset, you strive for continuous improvement and excellence in all your financial endeavors.

Power Moves to Make It Happen

1. Set High Standards:

- **Define Excellence:** Clearly outline what financial excellence looks like for you.
- **Aim High:** Set ambitious financial goals that challenge you to grow.

2. Develop a Strong Work Ethic:

- **Stay Committed:** Dedicate yourself fully to your financial plans and strategies.
- **Be Persistent:** Keep pushing forward, even when faced with obstacles.

3. Continuously Improve:

- **Seek Knowledge:** Regularly educate yourself

about advanced financial strategies and opportunities.

- **Adapt and Innovate:** Be open to new ideas and methods that can enhance your financial success.

4. Monitor and Evaluate:

- **Regular Reviews:** Assess your financial progress frequently to ensure you're on track.
- **Adjust Strategies:** Make necessary changes to your plans based on your evaluations.

Quick Reflection

- *"What does financial excellence mean to you?"*
- *"How can you push yourself to achieve higher standards in your finances?"*

29: I ATTRACT POSITIVE FINANCIAL INFLUENCES

Your Daily Boost

"I attract positive financial influences."

The Power Behind It

Attracting positive financial influences means surrounding yourself with people and environments that support and enhance your financial well-being. This affirmation helps you build a network that encourages your financial growth and provides valuable insights. With this mindset, you create a supportive ecosystem that fosters your financial success.

Power Moves to Make It Happen

1. Build a Supportive Network:

- **Connect with Like-Minded Individuals:** Engage with people who share your financial goals and values.
- **Join Financial Groups:** Participate in communities or forums that focus on financial growth and support.

2. Seek Positive Role Models:

- **Find Mentors:** Look up to individuals who have achieved financial success and learn from their experiences.
- **Follow Inspiring Leaders:** Follow financial experts and influencers who provide valuable

advice and motivation.

3. **Create a Positive Environment:**

   - **Surround Yourself with Positivity:** Keep your workspace and living areas filled with inspiring quotes and symbols of success.
   - **Limit Negative Influences:** Reduce exposure to negative financial news or pessimistic individuals who may hinder your progress.

4. **Share Your Goals:**

   - **Communicate Your Aspirations:** Let others know about your financial goals to gain their support and encouragement.
   - **Collaborate with Others:** Work together with others on financial projects or investments to enhance mutual success.

Quick Reflection

   - *"Who are the positive financial influences in your life?"*
   - *"How can you attract more supportive people to your financial journey?"*

30: I AM THE MASTER OF MY FINANCIAL DESTINY

Your Daily Boost

"I am the master of my financial destiny."

The Power Behind It

Being the master of your financial destiny means taking full responsibility for your financial future and actively shaping it through your decisions and actions. This affirmation empowers you to take control and make choices that align with your financial aspirations. With this mindset, you become proactive in creating the financial life you desire.

Power Moves to Make It Happen

1. Take Responsibility:

- **Own Your Finances:** Acknowledge that you are in control of your financial situation.
- **Avoid Blame:** Focus on what you can do to improve rather than blaming external factors.

2. Set Clear Financial Goals:

- **Define Your Vision:** Know exactly what you want to achieve financially.
- **Create a Plan:** Develop a detailed roadmap to reach your financial objectives.

3. Take Proactive Steps:

- **Make Informed Decisions:** Research and

analyze before making financial choices.

- **Act Consistently:** Regularly work towards your financial goals without procrastination.

4. Empower Yourself:

- **Seek Knowledge:** Continuously educate yourself about personal finance and investment strategies.
- **Build Confidence:** Trust in your ability to make the right financial decisions.

Quick Reflection

- *"In what ways are you currently mastering your financial destiny?"*
- *"What actions can you take today to take greater control of your financial future?"*

31: I CREATE VALUE AND RECEIVE ABUNDANCE

Your Daily Boost

"I create value and receive abundance."

The Power Behind It

When you focus on creating value, abundance naturally follows. This affirmation reminds you that by offering something meaningful, whether it's your time, skills, or resources, you open yourself up to receiving financial rewards. Embrace the idea that your contributions are valuable and that abundance is your natural reward.

Power Moves to Make It Happen

1. Identify Your Strengths:

- **Assess Your Skills:** Take stock of what you're good at and how you can use these skills to create value.
- **Leverage Your Talents:** Find ways to apply your strengths in your work or business to enhance your offerings.

2. Focus on Quality:

- **Deliver Excellence:** Ensure that everything you do is of high quality, making your work stand out.
- **Seek Feedback:** Ask others for their opinions to continuously improve your value proposition.

3. **Help Others:**

    - **Provide Solutions:** Look for ways to solve problems for others, adding real value to their lives.
    - **Be Generous:** Share your knowledge and resources freely to build trust and goodwill.

4. **Stay Consistent:**

    - **Maintain Standards:** Keep delivering value consistently to build a strong reputation.
    - **Persist Through Challenges:** Continue creating value even when faced with obstacles.

Quick Reflection

- *"How am I currently creating value in my life and work?"*
- *"What steps can I take today to increase the value I provide to others?"*

32: I AM DEDICATED TO BUILDING MY WEALTH

Your Daily Boost

"I am dedicated to building my wealth."

The Power Behind It

Dedication is the key to building lasting wealth. This affirmation reinforces your commitment to your financial goals, encouraging you to stay focused and persistent. With dedication, you overcome challenges and keep moving forward, steadily growing your wealth over time.

Power Moves to Make It Happen

1. Set Clear Financial Goals:

- **Define Your Targets:** Know exactly what you want to achieve financially, whether it's saving a certain amount or investing in a property.
- **Write Them Down:** Document your goals to keep them top of mind and track your progress.

2. Create a Financial Plan:

- **Budget Wisely:** Allocate your income towards savings, investments, and necessary expenses.
- **Plan for the Future:** Develop strategies for long-term financial growth and stability.

3. Stay Consistent:

- **Daily Habits:** Incorporate money-building activities into your daily routine, such as saving a portion of your income.

- **Avoid Procrastination:** Take immediate steps towards your financial goals instead of delaying.

4. **Educate Yourself:**

    - **Learn About Finances:** Read books, attend seminars, or take courses on wealth building and money management.

    - **Apply Knowledge:** Implement what you learn to make informed financial decisions.

Quick Reflection

- "What financial goals am I most dedicated to achieving?"

- "How can I strengthen my dedication to building my wealth today?"

33: I AM RESILIENT IN MY FINANCIAL JOURNEY

Your Daily Boost

"I am resilient in my financial journey."

The Power Behind It

Resilience allows you to bounce back from financial setbacks and keep moving forward. This affirmation strengthens your ability to handle challenges with grace and determination. By being resilient, you maintain your focus on your financial goals, no matter the obstacles that arise.

Power Moves to Make It Happen

1. Embrace a Growth Mindset:

- **Learn from Mistakes:** View financial setbacks as opportunities to grow and improve.
- **Stay Positive:** Focus on the lessons learned rather than the failures.

2. Develop a Support System:

- **Seek Guidance:** Connect with mentors or financial advisors who can offer advice and support.
- **Join Communities:** Engage with groups that share your financial goals and can provide encouragement.

3. Practice Stress Management:

- **Stay Calm:** Use techniques like deep breathing or meditation to manage financial stress.
- **Take Breaks:** Allow yourself time to rest and recharge when facing financial challenges.

4. Stay Flexible:

- **Adapt to Change:** Be willing to adjust your financial plans as needed to overcome obstacles.
- **Find Alternative Solutions:** Look for different ways to achieve your financial goals when faced with setbacks.

Quick Reflection

- *"How have I demonstrated resilience in my financial life recently?"*
- *"What strategies can I use to stay resilient during financial challenges?"*

34: I ATTRACT HIGH-PAYING OPPORTUNITIES

Your Daily Boost

"I attract high-paying opportunities."

The Power Behind It

Attracting high-paying opportunities means positioning yourself to receive better financial rewards. This affirmation helps you believe in your worth and seek out opportunities that offer greater compensation. By focusing on high-value opportunities, you enhance your potential for increased income and financial growth.

Power Moves to Make It Happen

1. Enhance Your Skills:

- **Continuous Learning:** Take courses or gain certifications to increase your expertise.
- **Stay Updated:** Keep up with industry trends to remain competitive and attractive to high-paying employers or clients.

2. Network Strategically:

- **Build Connections:** Attend industry events and connect with professionals who can lead you to lucrative opportunities.
- **Leverage Social Media:** Use platforms like LinkedIn to showcase your skills and attract potential employers or partners.

3. **Showcase Your Value:**

   - **Create a Strong Portfolio:** Highlight your achievements and the value you bring to potential opportunities.

   - **Communicate Effectively:** Clearly articulate your skills and how they can benefit others in interviews or pitches.

4. **Seek Out Opportunities:**

   - **Be Proactive:** Don't wait for opportunities to come to you; actively seek out high-paying roles or projects.

   - **Negotiate Wisely:** When presented with an opportunity, negotiate for the best possible compensation that reflects your worth.

Quick Reflection

- *"What high-paying opportunities am I currently attracting?"*

- *"How can I better position myself to attract more lucrative opportunities?"*

35: I AM FINANCIALLY FREE AND SECURE

Your Daily Boost

"I am financially free and secure."

The Power Behind It

Financial freedom and security provide peace of mind and the ability to live life on your own terms. This affirmation reinforces your commitment to achieving a stable and independent financial state. By believing in your financial security, you make choices that protect and grow your wealth, ensuring long-term stability.

Power Moves to Make It Happen

1. Build an Emergency Fund:

   - **Save Regularly:** Set aside a portion of your income each month for unexpected expenses.
   - **Set Goals:** Aim to save at least three to six months' worth of living expenses.

2. Eliminate Debt:

   - **Create a Debt Repayment Plan:** Prioritize paying off high-interest debts first.
   - **Avoid New Debt:** Be mindful of taking on new debts and manage existing ones responsibly.

3. Invest for the Future:

   - **Diversify Investments:** Spread your investments across different assets to reduce risk.

- **Plan for Retirement:** Contribute to retirement accounts to ensure financial security in the future.

4. **Live Within Your Means:**

    - **Budget Wisely:** Track your income and expenses to ensure you're not overspending.
    - **Prioritize Needs Over Wants:** Focus on essential expenses and save or invest the rest.

Quick Reflection

- *"What steps have I taken to achieve financial freedom and security?"*
- *"How can I further strengthen my financial security today?"*

36: I INVEST MY MONEY WISELY

Your Daily Boost

"I invest my money wisely."

The Power Behind It

Wise investing is crucial for growing your wealth and securing your financial future. This affirmation encourages you to make informed and strategic investment decisions. By investing wisely, you maximize your returns and build a strong financial foundation that supports your long-term goals.

Power Moves to Make It Happen

1. **Educate Yourself:**

   - **Learn the Basics:** Understand different types of investments such as stocks, bonds, real estate, and mutual funds.
   - **Stay Informed:** Keep up with financial news and trends to make informed investment choices.

2. **Diversify Your Portfolio:**

   - **Spread Your Investments:** Invest in a variety of assets to reduce risk and increase potential returns.
   - **Balance Your Portfolio:** Ensure a mix of high-risk and low-risk investments to stabilize your portfolio.

3. **Set Clear Investment Goals:**

- **Define Your Objectives:** Know what you want to achieve with your investments, such as saving for retirement or buying a home.

- **Create a Plan:** Develop a strategy that outlines how to reach your investment goals.

4. **Monitor and Adjust:**

   - **Regular Reviews:** Keep track of your investment performance and make adjustments as needed.

   - **Stay Flexible:** Be willing to change your investment strategy based on market conditions and personal goals.

Quick Reflection

- *"How am I currently investing my money wisely?"*

- *"What changes can I make to improve my investment strategy?"*

37: I AM OPEN TO RECEIVING FINANCIAL ABUNDANCE

Your Daily Boost

"I am open to receiving financial abundance."

The Power Behind It

Being open to receiving financial abundance means welcoming wealth into your life without hesitation or self-doubt. This affirmation helps you let go of limiting beliefs and embrace the flow of money and opportunities. By staying open, you allow abundance to enter your life in various forms, enhancing your financial well-being.

Power Moves to Make It Happen

1. **Release Limiting Beliefs:**

    - **Identify Barriers:** Recognize any negative thoughts that prevent you from accepting abundance.
    - **Replace with Positivity:** Affirm positive beliefs about money and your ability to receive it.

2. **Practice Gratitude:**

    - **Daily Gratitude:** Focus on what you're thankful for, which attracts more abundance.
    - **Appreciate Opportunities:** Acknowledge and celebrate financial gains, no matter how small.

3. **Visualize Abundance:**

    - **Daily Visualization:** Imagine yourself living

a life of financial abundance and feel the emotions associated with it.

- **Create a Vision Board:** Use images and words that represent financial abundance to inspire you daily.

4. Take Inspired Action:

- **Act on Opportunities:** When you feel inspired to take action towards financial goals, follow through.
- **Stay Receptive:** Be open to new ideas and opportunities that can bring financial abundance into your life.

Quick Reflection

- "How open am I to receiving financial abundance in my life?"
- "What can I do today to become more receptive to financial opportunities?"

38: I TRUST THE PROCESS OF WEALTH CREATION

Your Daily Boost

"I trust the process of wealth creation."

The Power Behind It

Trusting the process of wealth creation means having faith in your financial journey, even when progress seems slow. This affirmation reinforces your belief that consistent efforts and wise decisions will lead to financial success. By trusting the process, you stay patient and committed, allowing wealth to build over time.

Power Moves to Make It Happen

1. Be Patient:

- **Understand Timing:** Recognize that building wealth takes time and consistent effort.
- **Stay Committed:** Continue working towards your financial goals, even when results aren't immediate.

2. Focus on Long-Term Goals:

- **Set Milestones:** Break down your wealth creation into achievable milestones.
- **Celebrate Progress:** Acknowledge and celebrate each step you take towards your long-term goals.

3. Stay Consistent:

- **Regular Investments:** Make consistent investments to build your wealth steadily.
- **Maintain Good Habits:** Stick to your budget, save regularly, and avoid unnecessary expenses.

4. Let Go of Control:

- **Accept Uncertainties:** Understand that some factors in wealth creation are beyond your control.
- **Adapt and Adjust:** Be flexible and ready to adjust your strategies as needed without losing faith in the process.

Quick Reflection

- *"How do I stay patient and trust the wealth creation process?"*
- *"What long-term financial goals am I committed to achieving?"*

39: I AM A POWERFUL MONEY MAGNET

Your Daily Boost

"I am a powerful money magnet."

The Power Behind It

Being a powerful money magnet means attracting financial opportunities and wealth effortlessly. This affirmation boosts your confidence and aligns your mindset with abundance, making it easier to draw in money and prosperity. By believing in your ability to attract wealth, you position yourself to receive and manage money effectively.

Power Moves to Make It Happen

1. **Maintain a Positive Attitude:**

    - **Think Abundantly:** Focus on the positive aspects of your financial situation.
    - **Avoid Negativity:** Steer clear of negative thoughts that can repel wealth.

2. **Visualize Wealth:**

    - **Daily Visualization:** Imagine yourself surrounded by wealth and experiencing financial success.
    - **Feel the Emotions:** Let yourself feel the joy and security that comes with being financially abundant.

3. **Take Action Towards Wealth:**

- **Pursue Opportunities:** Actively seek out ways to increase your income and build your wealth.
- **Be Proactive:** Don't wait for money to come to you; take steps to attract it.

4. **Practice Gratitude:**

    - **Appreciate What You Have:** Regularly express gratitude for the money and opportunities you currently have.
    - **Invite More Abundance:** Gratitude attracts more wealth into your life.

Quick Reflection

- *"How do I embody the qualities of a money magnet?"*
- *"What actions can I take today to attract more wealth into my life?"*

40: I ATTRACT FINANCIAL MIRACLES

Your Daily Boost

"I attract financial miracles."

The Power Behind It

Attracting financial miracles means believing that extraordinary financial blessings are possible in your life. This affirmation encourages you to stay open to unexpected opportunities and blessings that can significantly impact your financial situation. By embracing the possibility of miracles, you invite transformative changes and abundance into your financial journey.

Power Moves to Make It Happen

1. Stay Open to Possibilities:

- **Embrace the Unexpected:** Be willing to consider unconventional or surprising financial opportunities.
- **Keep an Open Mind:** Don't limit yourself to traditional methods of earning and saving money.

2. Believe in Miracles:

- **Cultivate Faith:** Trust that financial miracles can happen to you.
- **Visualize Success:** Regularly imagine miraculous financial events happening in your life.

3. Take Inspired Action:

- **Act on Intuition:** Follow your gut feelings when it comes to financial decisions and opportunities.

- **Be Ready to Act:** When a miraculous opportunity arises, be prepared to take swift and decisive action.

4. Practice Generosity:

    - **Give Freely:** Share your wealth and resources with others, creating a flow of abundance.

    - **Receive Graciously:** Accept financial blessings and opportunities with gratitude and openness.

Quick Reflection

- *"What financial miracles have I experienced or witnessed in my life?"*

- *"How can I create space for more financial miracles to enter my life?"*

41: I AM COMMITTED TO MY FINANCIAL GROWTH

Your Daily Boost

"I am committed to my financial growth."

The Power Behind It

Commitment to your financial growth ensures you stay focused and dedicated to improving your financial situation. This affirmation strengthens your determination to learn, grow, and take actions that increase your wealth. With unwavering commitment, you turn your financial goals into reality.

Power Moves to Make It Happen

1. Set Clear Financial Goals:

- **Define Your Objectives:** Clearly outline what you want to achieve financially, whether it's saving for a house, investing in stocks, or building an emergency fund.

- **Write Them Down:** Document your goals to keep them top of mind and track your progress over time.

2. Create a Financial Plan:

- **Budget Wisely:** Allocate your income towards savings, investments, and necessary expenses to ensure balanced growth.

- **Plan for the Future:** Develop strategies that will help you reach your financial milestones, such as retirement planning or debt elimination.

3. Educate Yourself:

- **Learn About Finances:** Read books, attend seminars, or take online courses on money management and investing to expand your knowledge.

- **Apply Your Knowledge:** Implement the strategies you learn to make informed financial decisions that drive growth.

4. Stay Consistent:

- **Daily Habits:** Incorporate money-building activities into your daily routine, such as saving a portion of your income or tracking your expenses.

- **Avoid Procrastination:** Take immediate steps towards your financial goals instead of delaying, ensuring steady progress.

Quick Reflection

- *"What financial goals am I most dedicated to achieving?"*

- *"How can I strengthen my dedication to building my wealth today?"*

42: I DESERVE TO LIVE A WEALTHY LIFE

Your Daily Boost

"I deserve to live a wealthy life."

The Power Behind It

Believing that you deserve a wealthy life is fundamental to attracting abundance. This affirmation reinforces your self-worth and your right to financial success. When you acknowledge your deservingness, you open yourself up to opportunities that lead to a prosperous and fulfilling life.

Power Moves to Make It Happen

1. Embrace Self-Worth:

- **Acknowledge Your Value:** Recognize your skills, talents, and the unique contributions you bring to the table.
- **Positive Self-Talk:** Replace any negative beliefs about money with affirmations that highlight your worthiness of wealth.

2. Set Ambitious Goals:

- **Dream Big:** Don't limit your financial aspirations; aim high to unlock your full potential.
- **Create a Roadmap:** Develop a step-by-step plan to achieve your wealth goals, breaking them down into manageable tasks.

3. **Invest in Yourself:**
    - **Personal Development:** Take courses or attend workshops that enhance your skills and increase your earning potential.
    - **Health and Well-Being:** Maintain your physical and mental health to ensure you have the energy and focus to pursue wealth.

4. **Celebrate Successes:**
    - **Acknowledge Achievements:** Take time to celebrate your financial milestones, no matter how small.
    - **Reward Yourself:** Treat yourself when you reach your goals to reinforce your deservingness of wealth.

Quick Reflection

- "In what ways do I honor my worthiness of prosperity?"
- "What actions can I take today to reinforce my belief that I deserve a wealthy life?"

43: I AM ATTRACTING FINANCIAL ABUNDANCE DAILY

Your Daily Boost

"I am attracting financial abundance daily."

The Power Behind It

Attracting financial abundance daily means consistently inviting wealth into your life through your thoughts and actions. This affirmation keeps you focused on abundance, helping you recognize and seize opportunities that enhance your financial well-being. By maintaining this mindset, you create a continuous flow of prosperity.

Power Moves to Make It Happen

1. Practice Daily Affirmations:

- **Repeat Affirmations:** Say your financial abundance affirmation every morning and night to reinforce your mindset.
- **Believe in Your Words:** Truly feel the affirmation as you speak it, letting it shape your thoughts and actions.

2. Visualize Abundance:

- **Daily Visualization:** Spend a few minutes each day imagining yourself surrounded by wealth and financial success.
- **Create a Vision Board:** Use images and words that represent financial abundance to inspire and motivate you.

3. **Take Proactive Steps:**

   - **Seek Opportunities:** Actively look for ways to increase your income, such as side jobs or investment opportunities.
   - **Be Open to Change:** Embrace new methods and strategies that can lead to greater financial abundance.

4. **Cultivate Gratitude:**

   - **Gratitude Journal:** Write down things you're grateful for each day, especially related to your finances.
   - **Appreciate Small Wins:** Celebrate even the smallest financial successes to attract more abundance.

Quick Reflection

   - *"What financial abundance have I attracted today?"*
   - *"How can I continue to attract more wealth into my life each day?"*

44: I AM FINANCIALLY THRIVING

Your Daily Boost

"I am financially thriving."

The Power Behind It

Thriving financially means not just surviving but flourishing in your financial life. This affirmation encourages you to build a robust financial foundation and enjoy the prosperity you've worked hard to achieve. By believing in your ability to thrive, you set the stage for sustained financial success and well-being.

Power Moves to Make It Happen

1. Monitor Your Finances:

   - **Track Income and Expenses:** Keep a detailed record of where your money comes from and where it goes.
   - **Regular Reviews:** Assess your financial status monthly to stay on top of your financial health.

2. Invest in Growth:

   - **Smart Investments:** Allocate funds to investments that offer growth potential, such as stocks or real estate.
   - **Diversify:** Spread your investments across different assets to minimize risk and maximize returns.

3. Increase Your Income Streams:

- **Side Hustles:** Explore additional sources of income, such as freelance work or online businesses.

- **Passive Income:** Invest in opportunities that generate income with minimal ongoing effort, like rental properties or dividends.

4. Manage Debt Wisely:

    - **Reduce Debt:** Focus on paying down high-interest debts to free up more of your income for savings and investments.

    - **Avoid New Debt:** Be cautious about taking on new debt and ensure it aligns with your financial goals.

Quick Reflection

- *"In what ways am I currently thriving financially?"*

- *"What can I do today to enhance my financial thriving?"*

45: I EMBRACE A WEALTH-CONSCIOUS MINDSET

Your Daily Boost

"I embrace a wealth-conscious mindset."

The Power Behind It

Embracing a wealth-conscious mindset means consistently focusing your thoughts and actions on creating and maintaining wealth. This affirmation helps you stay mindful of your financial goals and encourages you to make decisions that support your abundance. With a wealth-conscious mindset, you align your daily habits with your long-term financial success.

Power Moves to Make It Happen

1. Stay Mindful of Spending:

- **Track Expenses:** Keep a close eye on where your money is going to ensure you're spending wisely.
- **Prioritize Needs:** Focus on essential expenses and limit spending on non-essentials.

2. Focus on Savings:

- **Automate Savings:** Set up automatic transfers to your savings account to ensure consistent saving.
- **Set Savings Goals:** Define clear targets for your savings to keep you motivated and on track.

3. Invest in Your Future:

- **Retirement Planning:** Contribute regularly to retirement accounts to secure your financial future.
- **Long-Term Investments:** Choose investments that will grow over time, providing lasting wealth.

4. Cultivate Positive Financial Habits:
    - **Daily Financial Review:** Spend a few minutes each day reviewing your financial status and goals.
    - **Continuous Learning:** Educate yourself about personal finance and investment strategies to enhance your wealth-building efforts.

Quick Reflection

- *"How does a wealth-conscious mindset influence my daily financial decisions?"*
- *"What positive financial habits can I develop to support my wealth mindset?"*

46: I AM A CREATOR OF FINANCIAL PROSPERITY

Your Daily Boost

"I am a creator of financial prosperity."

The Power Behind It

Creating financial prosperity means actively shaping your financial destiny through intentional actions and decisions. This affirmation empowers you to take charge of your financial future, fostering a proactive approach to building wealth. By seeing yourself as a creator, you embrace the responsibility and opportunity to generate prosperity in your life.

Power Moves to Make It Happen

1. Take Initiative:

- **Proactive Planning:** Develop and implement strategies to increase your income and grow your wealth.

- **Seek Opportunities:** Look for new ways to earn, invest, and save to build your financial prosperity.

2. Set and Achieve Goals:

- **Define Clear Goals:** Establish specific financial objectives that you want to achieve.

- **Create Action Plans:** Break down your goals into actionable steps and work towards them consistently.

3. **Invest in Personal Growth:**
   - **Enhance Skills:** Continuously improve your skills to increase your earning potential.
   - **Seek Knowledge:** Stay informed about financial trends and strategies to make informed decisions.

4. **Maintain a Positive Attitude:**
   - **Stay Optimistic:** Believe in your ability to create financial prosperity, even when faced with challenges.
   - **Overcome Obstacles:** Use setbacks as learning opportunities to strengthen your financial strategies.

Quick Reflection
- "What financial prosperity have I created in my life so far?"
- "How can I take more initiative to build my financial prosperity?"

47: I ATTRACT WEALTH EFFORTLESSLY

Your Daily Boost

"I attract wealth effortlessly."

The Power Behind It

Attracting wealth effortlessly means aligning your actions and mindset to bring abundance into your life with ease. This affirmation helps you believe that wealth is a natural part of your existence, reducing resistance and making it easier to receive financial blessings. By embracing this effortless attraction, you create a seamless flow of money and opportunities into your life.

Power Moves to Make It Happen

1. Align Your Actions with Abundance:

- **Take Inspired Action:** Act on opportunities that feel right and aligned with your financial goals.
- **Stay Open-Minded:** Be receptive to new and unexpected ways wealth can enter your life.

2. Let Go of Limiting Beliefs:

- **Identify Blocks:** Recognize any negative thoughts or beliefs that hinder your ability to attract wealth.
- **Replace with Positivity:** Use affirmations and positive self-talk to eliminate limiting beliefs.

3. Practice Gratitude:

- **Daily Gratitude:** Focus on what you're thankful for, which attracts more wealth into your life.
- **Appreciate Abundance:** Regularly acknowledge and celebrate the wealth you already have.

4. **Maintain a Positive Vibe:**

    - **Positive Environment:** Surround yourself with positivity through uplifting music, books, and people.
    - **Energy of Abundance:** Emit positive energy that attracts financial prosperity effortlessly.

Quick Reflection

- "How do I embody the effortless attraction of wealth in my daily life?"
- "What can I do today to make attracting wealth easier and more natural?"

48: I AM IN CONTROL OF MY FINANCIAL FUTURE

Your Daily Boost

"I am in control of my financial future."

The Power Behind It

Being in control of your financial future means taking responsibility and actively managing your finances to achieve your goals. This affirmation empowers you to make informed decisions and steer your financial life in the direction you desire. With control, you create a secure and prosperous future for yourself and your loved ones.

Power Moves to Make It Happen

1. Take Ownership:

- **Manage Your Finances:** Take charge of your income, expenses, savings, and investments.
- **Avoid Blame:** Focus on what you can control and take responsibility for your financial situation.

2. Plan Strategically:

- **Set Financial Goals:** Define clear, achievable goals for your financial future.
- **Develop a Roadmap:** Create a step-by-step plan to reach your financial objectives.

3. Make Informed Decisions:

- **Research Thoroughly:** Gather all necessary

information before making financial choices.

- **Evaluate Options:** Consider the pros and cons of each decision to ensure it aligns with your goals.

4. **Stay Disciplined:**

   - **Stick to Your Budget:** Follow your financial plan diligently to stay on track.

   - **Avoid Impulse Spending:** Make thoughtful purchases that support your long-term financial goals.

Quick Reflection

- *"How am I currently taking control of my financial future?"*

- *"What steps can I take today to strengthen my control over my finances?"*

49: I AM WORTHY OF ALL THE WEALTH I DESIRE

Your Daily Boost

"I am worthy of all the wealth I desire."

The Power Behind It

Believing that you are worthy of wealth is essential for attracting and maintaining financial abundance. This affirmation reinforces your self-worth and your right to enjoy the prosperity you seek. When you feel deserving, you are more likely to pursue opportunities and make decisions that lead to the wealth you desire.

Power Moves to Make It Happen

1. Cultivate Self-Worth:

- **Acknowledge Your Value:** Recognize your strengths and the unique qualities that make you deserving of wealth.
- **Positive Self-Talk:** Replace negative thoughts with affirmations that highlight your worthiness.

2. Set Ambitious Financial Goals:

- **Dream Big:** Don't limit your financial aspirations; aim high to unlock your full potential.
- **Create a Plan:** Develop a detailed strategy to achieve your wealth goals, breaking them down into actionable steps.

3. **Invest in Your Future:**

    - **Save and Invest:** Allocate funds towards savings and investments that will grow your wealth over time.
    - **Plan for Retirement:** Ensure you have a solid plan in place for financial security in your later years.

4. **Surround Yourself with Positivity:**

    - **Positive Environment:** Create a space that inspires and motivates you to achieve your financial goals.
    - **Supportive People:** Engage with individuals who uplift and encourage your financial journey.

Quick Reflection

- "How do I demonstrate my worthiness of wealth in my daily life?"
- "What actions can I take today to reinforce my belief that I deserve financial abundance?"

50: I AM CONTINUOUSLY ATTRACTING FINANCIAL OPPORTUNITIES

Your Daily Boost

"I am continuously attracting financial opportunities."

The Power Behind It

Continuously attracting financial opportunities means remaining open and receptive to new ways to grow your wealth. This affirmation keeps you alert to potential income streams and investment chances that can enhance your financial status. By maintaining this mindset, you ensure a steady flow of opportunities that contribute to your financial success.

Power Moves to Make It Happen

1. Stay Open-Minded:

- **Embrace New Ideas:** Be willing to consider unconventional or innovative ways to earn and invest money.
- **Adapt to Change:** Adjust your strategies as new opportunities arise to maximize your financial growth.

2. Network Regularly:

- **Build Connections:** Attend events and engage with professionals who can introduce you to new financial opportunities.
- **Leverage Relationships:** Use your network to

discover and pursue lucrative ventures.

3. **Enhance Your Skills:**

   - **Continuous Learning:** Invest in your education to stay competitive and attractive to high-paying opportunities.

   - **Diversify Skills:** Expand your expertise to open doors to various financial opportunities.

4. **Take Initiative:**

   - **Proactive Seeking:** Actively look for and pursue opportunities that align with your financial goals.

   - **Be Prepared:** Have a plan in place to take advantage of opportunities as they arise, ensuring you're ready to act quickly.

Quick Reflection

- *"What new financial opportunities have I attracted recently?"*

- *"How can I stay proactive in attracting more financial opportunities moving forward?*

CONCLUSION: IGNITE YOUR JOURNEY TO FINANCIAL FREEDOM

Embrace Your Wealth Mindset

Congratulations! You've reached the end of this transformative journey through powerful affirmations designed to reshape your financial reality. Each chapter has equipped you with the mindset and tools needed to attract abundance and achieve financial freedom. Now, it's time to put these affirmations into action and watch your financial dreams unfold.

Believe in Your Potential

Always remember that the power to create wealth lies within you. Believe in your ability to attract and manage abundance. You deserve a life filled with financial security and prosperity. Trust in yourself and the positive changes you're making. Your belief is the foundation upon which your financial success will be built.

Take Immediate Action

Don't wait for the perfect moment—start today! Every small step you take now brings you closer to your financial goals. Implement the power moves you've learned, stay dedicated, and maintain a positive, wealth-conscious mindset. The sooner you act, the sooner you'll begin to see the results of your efforts.

Stay Persistent and Resilient

The path to financial freedom may have its challenges, but your resilience will keep you moving forward. Stay committed to your goals, overcome obstacles with grace, and adapt to changes with flexibility. Your persistence is the key to turning setbacks into comebacks and maintaining steady progress toward your financial aspirations.

Keep the Fire Alive

Let the affirmations you've embraced continue to inspire and motivate you every day. Surround yourself with positivity, celebrate your achievements, and keep your financial goals in clear view. By maintaining this enthusiasm and focus, you ensure that your journey toward wealth remains vibrant and unstoppable.

Your Financial Freedom Awaits

The journey to financial freedom is yours to embark on. With a powerful mindset, consistent action, and unwavering belief in yourself, you can attract the abundance you deserve. Take control of your financial destiny today and step confidently into a future filled with prosperity and success.

Final Affirmation

"I am ready to take action and create the wealth and financial freedom I deserve."

Embrace this affirmation as your guiding star. Let it fuel your determination and keep you aligned with your financial goals. Your financial freedom is not just a distant dream—it's your reality waiting to be realized. Believe in yourself, take decisive action, and watch as your wealth mindset transforms your life.

By integrating these affirmations and power moves into your daily life, you are setting the stage for lasting abundance and financial independence. Stay positive, remain proactive, and continue believing in your ability to create the wealth and prosperity you deserve. Your journey to financial freedom starts now—ignite the fire within and make your dreams come true!

YOUR VOICE MATTERS — LEAVE A REVIEW

If this book made a positive impact on your life—whether it was a small insight or a complete shift—I'd be incredibly grateful if you could share your experience in a review on Amazon.

Your words might be just what someone else needs to begin their own journey. By sharing your thoughts on Amazon, you're not only helping others find it but showing how these strategies can truly make a difference.

Thank you for being part of this journey and for taking a moment to leave a review—your feedback means more than you know!

UNLOCK EXCLUSIVE FREE TOOLS & ARTICLES!

Visit www.theVishalAnand.com to instantly access a collection of powerful, free resources crafted to accelerate your journey to success. Discover actionable strategies, expert insights, and transformative tools—all at no cost—to help you overcome obstacles and unlock your true potential.

Start Your Transformation Today!

Printed in Dunstable, United Kingdom

65433561R00067